remains

EMAAN ABDUL WAHID

~~A collection of words that remains unchanged~~

~~The words that began the change~~

~~A collection of thoughts in my brain~~

~~The thoughts that couldn't be tamed~~

~~A collection of words forever engraved in my brain~~

~~Words that I failed to entertain~~

~~the silent flames that remain untamed~~

re·mains

~~the silent flames that remain untamed~~

~~A collection that drove me insane~~

~~A collection of worldly games~~

~~A collection of my complains~~

~~The words of hearts in pain~~

~~A collection of words disdained~~

~~A collection of words of someone in pain.~~

~~A collection of words never meant the same~~

ISBN: 978-9948-774-05-1

To the unspoken words and missed opportunities

Contents

You

Since the very beginning
Or as far as I can remember.
I had always loved you.
Specifically, when you walked in
on the 1st of December.

It was "love at first sight"
they would say, but I
was never good with words.
so, I drew away to be heard.
But I had lost my chance,
You were swept away in a glance,
But as you showed up with your heart in your hands
Wounded and wet with tears that weren't mine.
I couldn't say no,
As words were never mine.

So, I drew you a heart.
One filled with love from within
As drawing was the only language
I conversed in
But perhaps it was a foreign one,
One that couldn't be heard,
One that you'd never know,
One to be left unheard.

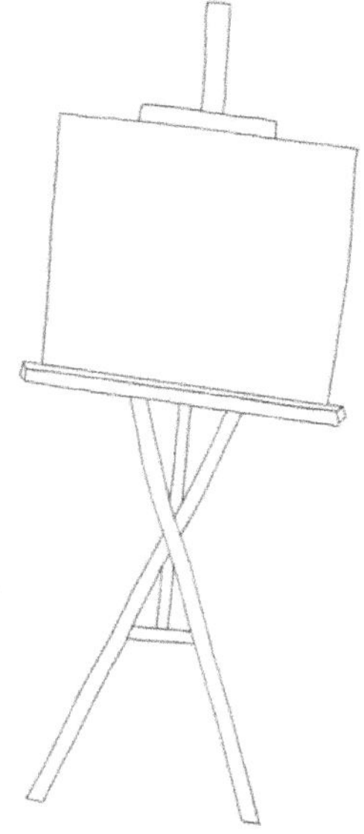

Loving in silence

I loved you in silence.
For what wouldn't hurt me

Is what you'd never know.

Answers

I look in your eyes,

With hope that you

Unseal all veracity.

That hides behind the seal

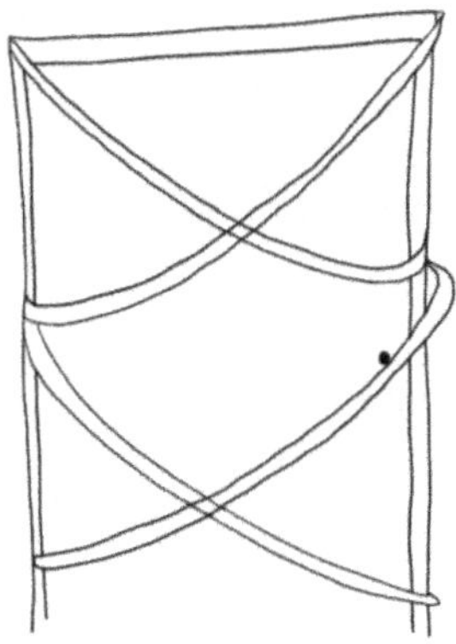

Longing

Every day she waited,
waited for hours for him to come home.
knowing that when he does
He will not be alone.
but at least she'd get to see him, right?
at least she'll know he's safe.
in the arms of someone who loves him
even if they could never love the same.

Every day she waited.
hours soon turned into days.
days when she would starve herself,
to match the inner cave

by now she was good at waiting
So, when he told her to wait.
she said yes.
Certain. It was worth the wait.

but minutes soon turned into hours,
hours soon turned into days,
days turned into months,
and a whole revolution in space
but he never came back.

So, she waited.
waited for hours for him to come home.
hoping that when he does
she will not be so alone.

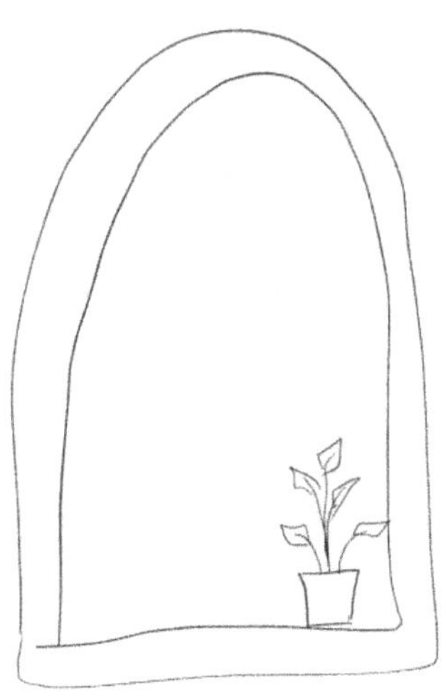

Not mine

I cannot have you
The words stuck in my chest
My tongue betrays me
But my mind knows the best.
You have that smile,
The words,
The face,
The eyes.
But ironically, *she* has your eyes.

"Did you see the way she looked at me?"
"We totally locked eyes!!!"

No, but if I hear about it one more time I might actually cry.
But I say nothing.
Just laugh and nod at the words
Because in through the ear and out the eyes they submerge.
I really like you.
But I know that you don't
It's her that you like
So, there is no "s" in front of u.
But there is always "her" before "me"
And you would give anything to maintain her glee

It's blinding really, just not blinding enough
But I pretend it is and I let myself burn
I am scared to meet your eyes
If I pretend long enough, I'll blink 'us 'into Life
I refuse to meet your eyes
Because if I do ,
that would mean goodbye

Dream

I close my eyes with a smile.
For at least in my dreams
You are mine

For a while

The ghost of you

I saw you smiling with your pretty eyed smile.
Your eyes staring right back at mine
Laughing about something I said the other day
Shining like the stars kept in line.

But you haven't stopped smiling in a while.
Only to have realized that the clocks had expired.

The time had stopped
But where was the wind that followed?
The time had stopped
Leaving me hollowed.

But I know this wasn't real
None of it was.
Cause how can you love someone
When they aren't living
At all.

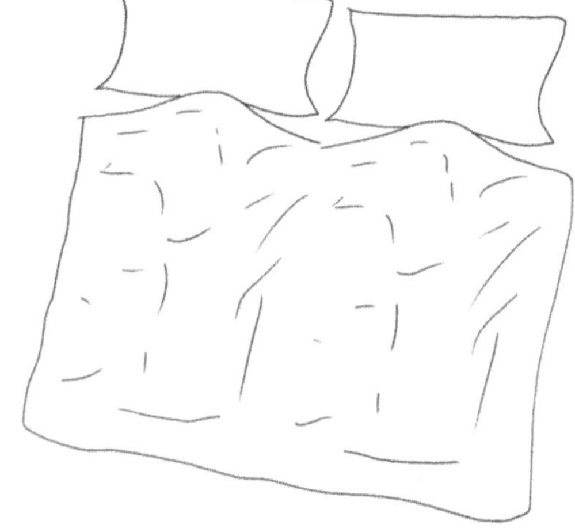

Contemporary

It's funny
how we thought we'd last.
Even swore
We'd be each other's last
Said the starts aligned only to whisper.
"It's written in the stars"

I really hoped we'd last.
Swore and crossed my heart.
Wished upon a star.
Hoping 11:11 would make it last.

But alas, it was only temporary.
As forever was never contemporary.

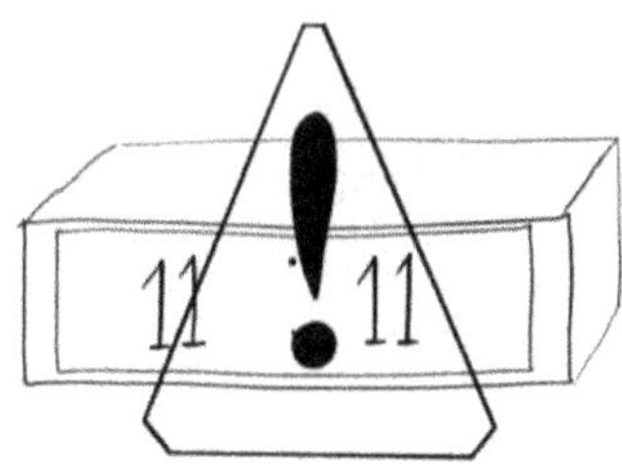

Haunt

"Ghosts are scary"
At least that's what we've been told
They haunt and make your
life a foretold

"Ghosts make you scream "
This one more in pain than fear
As your heart gets haunted
by someone you hold dear

"Ghosts are scary to look at"
I might look little surprised
For God took the stars and
said here are your eyes.

"Ghosts sounds horrible "
I close my eyes tight
For you sang my favorite melody
Every.single.night

"Ghosts can't be touched"
That one might be true
For I tried to hug you
But always went through

"Ghosts are meant to be scary"
But you are the only thing I refuse to let go.
For life took everything
And I can't let it take this too.

"Ghosts aren't humans"
I wish I wouldn't know.
For the ghost of you
Is all I've ever known.

Love(ed)

I did *love* you with all that I had.

But now I add an '*ed*' to that.

Impossible

Some people are easy to love,
But some?
Impossible to hate.
And that is when
Hearts began to
Break.

Sorry?

you looked at me then,
over the countless heads,
smiled a little crooked.
but smiled, nonetheless.

you seem to do that quite a lot
disappear for a while,
only to return with that smile.
You expect me to accept.
expect me to smile back.
and like a fool I did
for quite a while.

But this fool was in love,
this fool would have given you the world.
this fool would've welcomed you every day,
without asking for much.

but this fool is tired.
but a fool, nonetheless.
it ignores how your dictionary is too thin and unkept.
cause this fool forgives,
every time you whisper those words
and hates how the cycle somehow
keeps getting worse.

now this fool feels nauseous.
having fed the same words
over and over
until digesting became worse

and this fool is now sick.
but a fool, nonetheless.
cause this fool smiles back.
And whispers "I forgive"

Blind

I could never understand how animals
could be so gullible and fall for
something that was quite visible.

Be the cheese on a mouse trap
Or even, as big as bear traps.
How could they be so blind?
To the things that were right
Infront of them all this time

But I was better off unlearned,
As I now watch my heart get burned

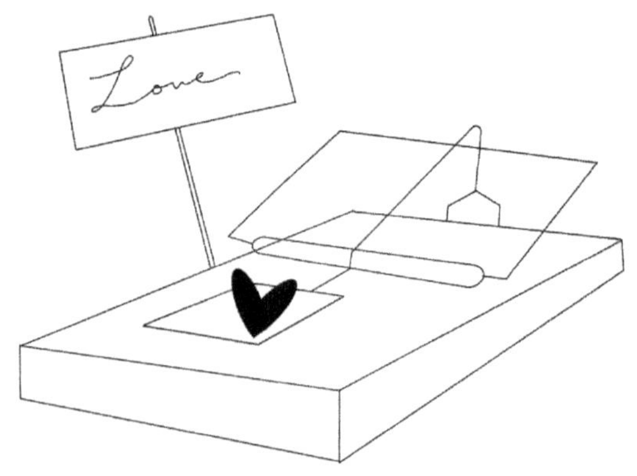

Expectations

maybe that's where we went wrong

we should have sung the song

instead,

we hummed and hoped

the other wouldn't get it wrong

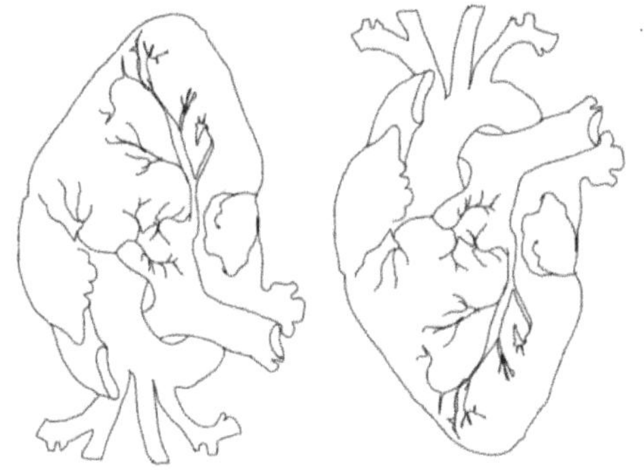

Right person, wrong time

People say right person wrong time isn't real.

They say if a person's right for you, times no big deal

But they'd know it if they saw us.

We were right for each other.

fitting together like two pieces of puzzle.

Failing to realize

We weren't part of the same puzzle.

One last time.

One last time
I want to see you face to face
Both at loss of words
Too many things I want to say
One last time
I smile and you smile back
A tiny acknowledgment of whatever that we had
One last time
I want to brush my hands against yours
Cause in all these years we never once crossed that road
One last time
I want to breathe you in
As far as my lungs would let you stay within
One last time
I wish that you were mine
One last time
You smiled and waved goodbye

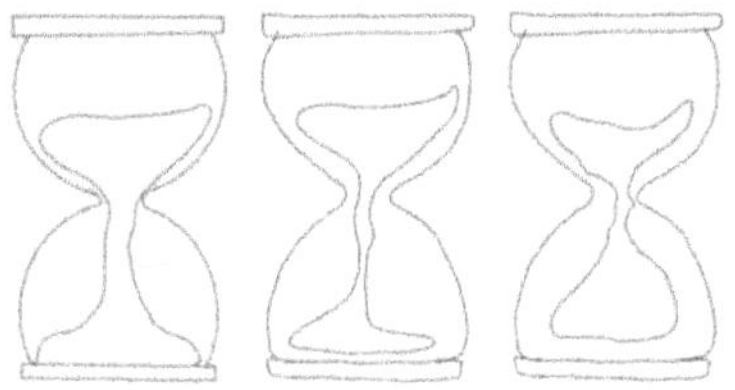

I hope you're happy

I hope you're happy.
Content with whom you chose.
I hope she makes you laugh,
Never letting a moment go.

I hope she takes you dancing,
And buys you flowers.
So, she doesn't have to listen to Bruno mars,
While crying in the showers.

I hope she makes you happy.
I hope you never stop smiling.
And I can see that she does,
The lines kind of describing.

I hope you got what you wanted.
The home you always longed for,
Cause I couldn't offer you the world.
Just someone to hold on to

I tried to make you stay,
I tried to make it work,
But the angels whispered,
'An error has occurred'.

I saw you leave then.
I tried to close my eyes.
But all I could see were the stars inside your eyes.
the smile on your lips,
the hand in your hand.
Which eventually,
Buried mine
in the sand.

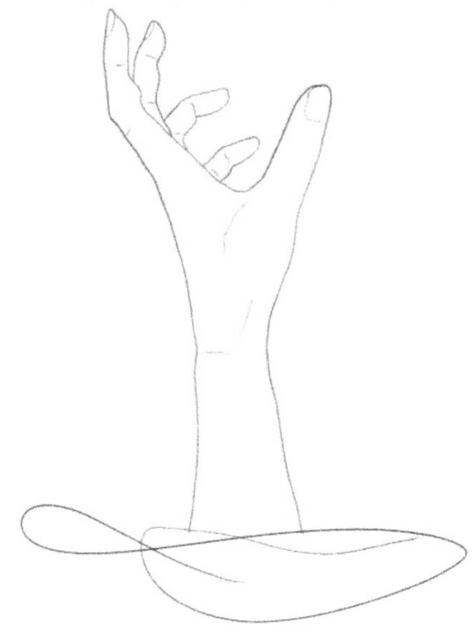

Almost

The first time I saw you
I knew I had to meet you
Planning to jump over the tracks
But the train had to stop too
Frantically searching your face
Trying to see you through
But when that train left you left with it too

The next time I was better
Almost close enough to know
where you stood and where you'd always go
'Hi' I said,
'Hey' you replied.
And that was the start
Of a never-ending ride

We became friends
We met each other frequently
Clicked almost like magnets
Pinching myself to check the reality

We always spoke for hours
Not that I would ever mind not even when the sun would rise
Cause you loved sunrises and well I, loved you
So, what a shame if we slept,
So, we saw that too

Going to the movies,
Cuddling and hanging out,
Our hands brushing while we walked,
Almost reached out.

The winter came by
Huddling close to keep us warm
Hot chocolates and cookies
Your voice, my favorite sound

We went out that day,
The food got on your lips
But before I could reach,
You licked it off your lips.

You're clumsy
But you never fell
It wasn't like the movies
Where I'd catch you and break the spell

Until one day I decided to tell you all about it
Tell you how my heart beats only when you're around it
Tell how I can't differentiate between fiction and reality
Ask you how you're real and not my mind playing reality

I ring the bell, hiding behind the flowers
My heart is in my throat,
No ribcage to protect it now.
Unprotected and raw
Ready to jump in your arms
You open the door,

But oh
You are not alone.

My heart drops back
Way down a pit made that fast

I was almost close
I am always almost close
I was almost close to wipe your lips
I was almost close to catch your trips
I was almost close to holding your hand
I was almost close to whispering be mine
I was almost close to dying right then
My heart almost stopped at the sight to take in

I was almost close
Almost to everything I guess
So, when I closed my eyes
I knew death almost felt like this

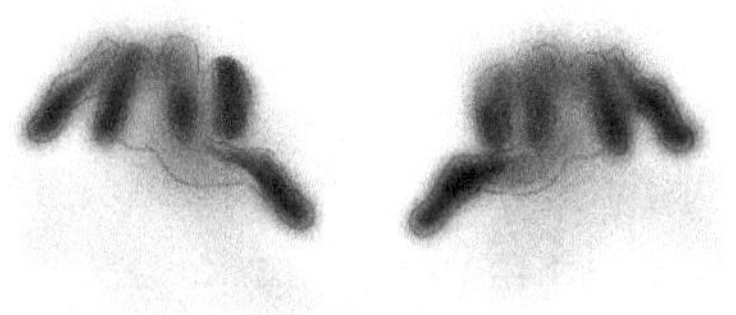

Left here

And when u left that day
(Contradictory to the saying)
My soul never did
it stayed right where you left it
Glued by its feet
Even as I eventually walked
Even as I screamed
You never turned back
Not even when I plead

So no,
you never took a piece of
my soul with you
But it did jump right out
Tried to reach for you
But only met drought

So no,
you didn't take a piece of me with you
But you did lead it astray
To a path where
Now
No one ever stays

When the clock strikes

The world is a cruel place.
beautiful but cruel
like beauty and the beast
except this is beast within beauty

in order to survive this,
mesmerizing yet pain arising world.
we must all be cured by
an intoxication and mesmerizing 'yours'

someone you can listen to for hours and hours,
even if the world gets devoured.
someone to call home,
even if the locations unknown.
Someone who silences the silence.
And makes the tabs close one by one.
Someone who makes you feel less human.
Someone you can call a conclusion.
Someone that is too good to be real,
That you joke about how he might not even be real.

But the world is a cruel place.
Beautiful but cruel
Maybe that's why he disappears,
every day for years,
as soon as the clock gears 10
He goes back to the den.

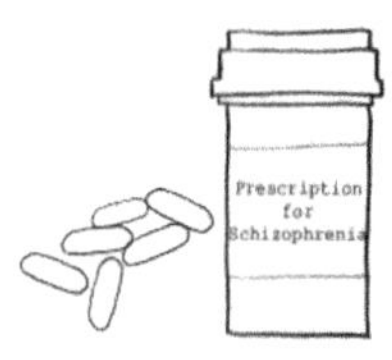

Wrong play

When someone told me I could live life like a movie
I didn't know the selection would be random,
Or that the previous years would be taken into consideration.
I thought I could audition for those cheesy romance movies,
Or even a funny comedic one.
But to my surprise I was chosen for none.

I tried contacting the director.
I screamed and screamed that I've been wronged.
But then the realization had hit
That the play had already begun
I became silent refusing to play the script.
But somehow the improvising only got more hits.

People come and go.
Praising the show
Some even crying, their lovers on their toes.
I sit through it all.
Watching the lovers pass
But there's nothing I can do.
As that's what the play's all about.

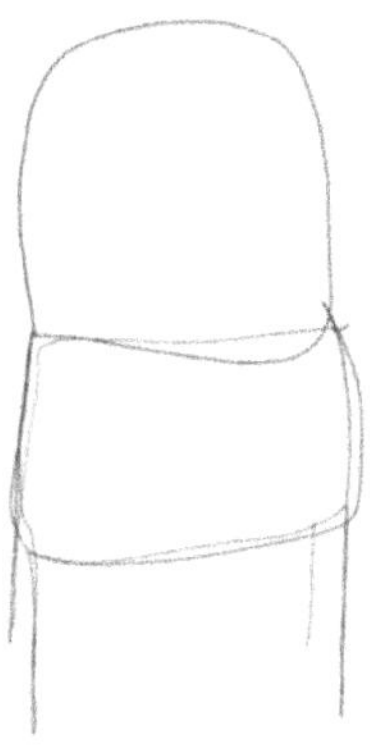

Am I ever going to get better?

Where does this pain come from?
I do not understand.
How to make it go away
was the plan.
I do not wish for it to stay.
But somehow,
I feel no other way.

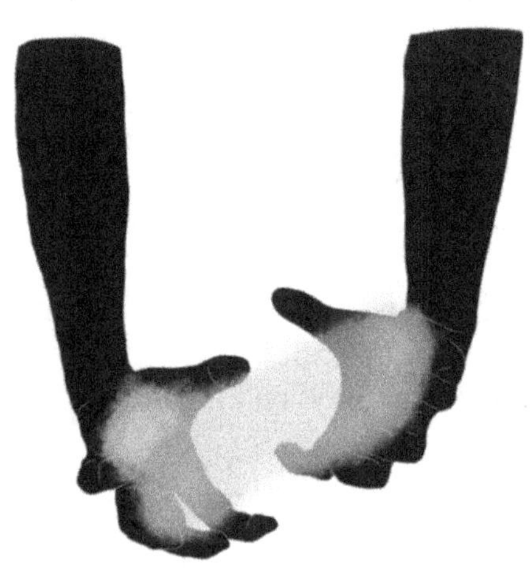

Who?

And am I supposed to turn when you call my name?
For I don't recognize myself
Just a body with a name

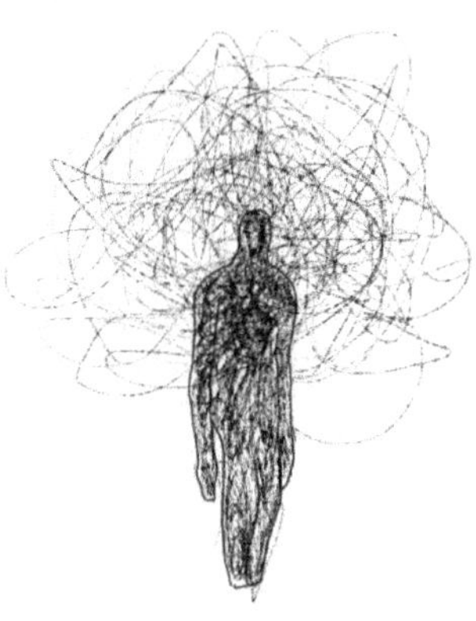

Journey

Here I am.
In the midst of it all
Skinned and stoned.
A walking corpse

Hope

I keep holding onto this stupid hope that I can't detach
myself away from.
If I could reach right inside me
And pull it out of its roots.
I would.
I would do it, but my hands
do not remember its owner.
My voice is muffled,
Under the thousand echoes.
And my eyes?
My eyes are blinded by hopeless visions.
Visions of what if?
Visions of a hopefully altered reality.
Visions of a multiverse, a universe

Hopefully
A better version
Of myself

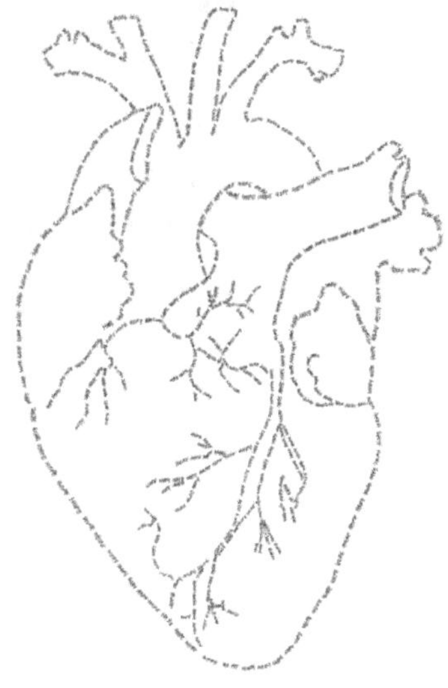

Who is this?

But what would happen
when this mask falls
What would happen
when the walls shatter down
Would u recognize me?
Or Wonder who this is
Or would there be no one?
Just a dry and empty field

Mourning

Why do I mourn for someone I never really had.

Want

Should wanting always hurt this bad?

To whomever it may concern

I cannot wait to have you.
Whoever you are, wherever you are.
Whether I have known you or if you are unknown
I can't wait to hug you.
To finally let go
To finally let myself go
I want all the cliche things I read about.
Let the eyes do the speaking but also let the words out.
I want the slow mornings with breakfast in bed.
Just us cuddled up, bed head.
I want the long walks, hand in hand.
And when there's thunder you just know where to stand.
I want to look at you.
All of you
I want to drink in your presence and never let go.
I want the silence. Just staring at your soul
Cause when something's so beautiful, you don't want to let
the moment go.
I want to be selfish, have you all to myself.
But I am scared I'll never have that,

not even a tiny glimpse.

0'o clock

Do you remember?
Remember the walk through the parks or
when you left me in the dark?

Or our marks on the bark,
Left untouched in the dark?

Or the spark in your eyes,
Or when it had died?

Or your pretty eyed smile,
That was never mine to pride.
Besides, will it ever subside?
Or will it haunt me
Until the day that it dies.

But that's uncertain,
Completely far-fetched.
Cause our initials are,
etched at a bark far west.

Or was I just a guest?
Addressed and wished best.

Or was I just a guest?
In the heart of whom I loved the best.

Remember 0'o clock?
Or should I say when the time had stopped.

Maybe it wasn't far-fetched.
As its *etched on a gravestone*
Far down the west

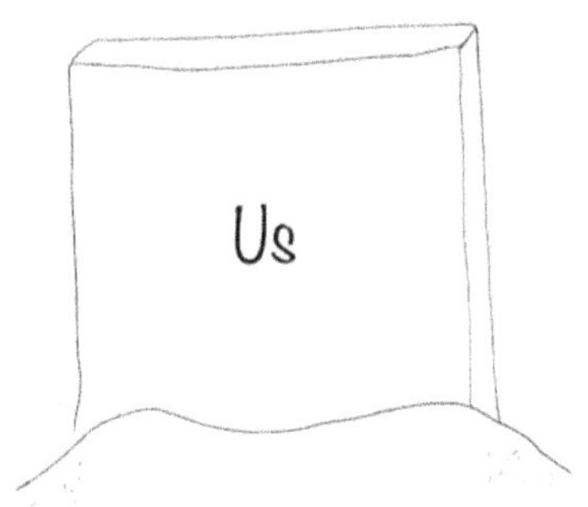

Betrayal

I had this fear I remember telling you about.
About people
Just being near me for their needs
Or simply just being because if not me then who else?

I remember telling you about this.
On a rooftop one summer night.
Just us and the night sky.

You took a few minutes just staring at my side.
And then blew out a deep breathe
And whispered that's not right.
You told me all about "How pretty I am"
And how my eyes shine when I speak about something that I
enjoy
Or how you love my downward smile.

You told me, but more than that
I had a heart of gold.
And my soul was probably made of something old.
You told me I forgive.
You told me that I give
You told me how I outlive
Anyone you've ever perceived

You told me I'm like gravity
Invisible to the eyes
But my presence speaks louder
Then any words could ever try.

You looked at me then your eyes not leaving mine
And you whispered that I'll always be fine.
I fell more deeply for you that day.
My fears not ever miles near you.
I had forgotten other people
Cause if I knew the sun why would I ever be scared to burn?

But I forgot that the Sun is hot,
I forgot that it burns,
I forgot that it rips your skin piece by piece,
Not once feeling concerned.

I felt that gut wrenching pain that day
Somewhere deep inside
Somewhere so deep its location wasn't precise.
I remember your words, which I thought were far from lies
But you just had to prove my fears were about right.
I didn't confront you
Instead, I let you go
Cause deep down I knew
Everyone would always go.

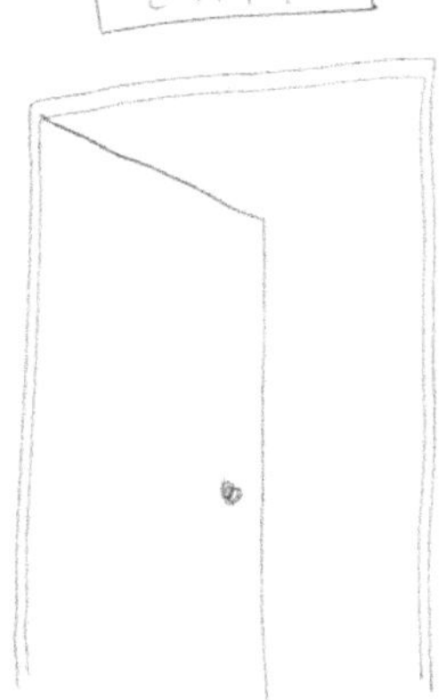

My name

When asked if you ever lost.

I hope my name is your first thought.

Riptide

And when asked about pain,
I hope you're clueless
Like when asked about tide currents
A topic you think is useless.

But for those who do know
Know,
When caught in a riptide,
One can only let it flow.

Let go

For when it gets too much. Let it go.

Just like the clouds when it rains.

one can only hold so much

Take it away.

You take the pain away.
The pain of never being enough

My home

Even though we're miles apart

My home is built within your heart

Him

He had the eyes
You could get lost into
Eyes that spoke so much
That books were jealous too

Silent understanding

What did we have?
The question still exists
Even though this is the last year we'd ever even exist.
Those one second glances
The smiles upon turns
The giddiness that's filled followed by something stupid that
you'd done
The incomplete sentences
The silent understanding
You opening the door, and me not sparing you those glances
The tiny gestures, I see you making way
Doing something for me that you'd know
I'd despicably hate.

You made sure to put space.
"Oh, she doesn't like close spaces"
But how would you know that
if we never shared those phrases.
You bring me my favorite chocolate
"Oh, I had this extra, please don't mind "
I gladly took it, savoring each bite
I kept the wrapper, not knowing the reason why
I guess I wanted to keep something to remember you by.
But my brain doesn't need remembering you're kind of
etched deep deep in.
That all it can manage is think where you've been?

The breathless from having you so close
You leaning down so you could hear me some more.
The staring into my soul
Your eyes, a sight for sure
The feeling of comfort.
Choosing you in a room full
Knowing that we'd understand
No words needed use

Iloveyou.

then the realization hits that I love you

that in a room full of people

my eyes find yours

that I always will love you.

regardless of what happens or where this goes.

cause my soul knows you.

And you have read mine too

And 'home' is what it calls you.

Not just another person it knew.

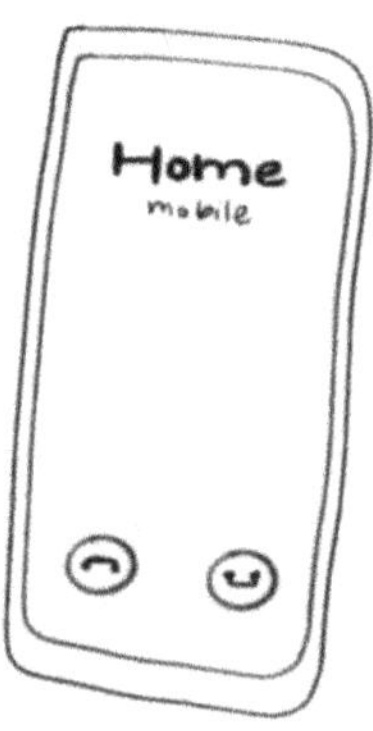

Can I love you ?

I want to love.
Not in the superficial kind of way
In the way it makes my heart ache every time you're away.
I want you close. In a way, defy ways,
1 body not 2 that close kind of way.
I want to hold hands, swinging side to side.
And when we walk on a path you pull to switch sides.
I want the late-night drives,
Blasting music windows down.
And we both have each other's playlist.
To listen when one's not around
The hand around my waist
Holding me close like I would break.
the 'this reminded me of you',
annotating books on the go
the I love you letters ,
no matter how old we shall grow.
I want to love.
love you.
Today and evermore

Vow

I cannot say I love you.
The uncertainties hold me back.
So, I show you everything that I have.

Your eyes were my favorite part.
How do they shine like that I ask?
You laughed and whispered
"For they carry you in their hearts"

You laughed.
And that was a song picked by heart.
Your laugh,
Was my favorite sound in the world.
But I would be lying if I said
my name by you wouldn't come first

Your gaze,
It leaves my mind in haze,
Uncertain and kind of feeling a little insane.

But my heart is something
I thought you'd never understand.
It speaks a language
You didn't know that you can.
It's something quite new, something that needs getting used to.
So will you hold my heart,
Till yours feel the same way too?

I love holding your hand,
Fitting perfectly against mine,
Would it be cliché if I said
'It was made to be mine'.

Maybe it's time I took the risk.
For every cliché movie starts with what if.
Maybe this isn't real,
Maybe we're in a book,
But we should be fine as long as it's a happy ending trope.

So,
To the one that has my heart.
Will you be mine and
Let death do us part?

Ruined.

I think of you when awake,

I dream of you whether it's night or day.

You consume me, and yet I am not afraid.

How have I lived all these years I cannot understand,

but now that I have met you, I do not think that I can.

I cannot not be near you.

and I cannot help but call your name.

You have ruined me,

in the most heavenly way one can be ruined.

Yours

I love you
I want to scream I love you
I want to climb the tallest building
and let my voice break through
I want to scream it so loud that the silence after is just as
deafening if not more
I want to say it to everyone
announce it to the world
but when I face u
I want to whisper you those words

I love you

I think I want to scream again.
But I jump into your arms instead
And you hug me so tight
Nothing was left unsaid

The moon

For I talk to the moon every night

In hushed whispers

I tell her about you

And she listens to it

Until the sky turns blue

Infinite

No matter where,
No matter when,
In my heart and mind,
Your name chants
Like the stars
Infinite amount of times

I will always love you.

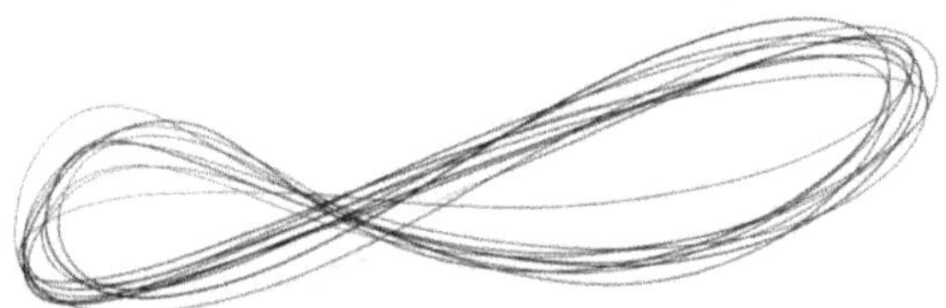

Where are you?

I wrote these words for you.
Knowing you exist they'll keep searching for you.
.

.

Someone that they miss.

remains- the silent flames that stay untamed

Acknowledgements

I would like to thank my parents and especially my siblings who listened to me go on and on about my ideas, thoughts and feelings at odd parts of the day, without whom none of this would be possible. I would also like to thank my best friend whose encouragement meant a lot to me.

I would also like to send my heart out to all poets and authors who have inspired me to be the writer I aspire to be. Who made me feel seen and heard just by their writings.

And lastly, I would also like to thank you for exploring a part of my soul with me, these were a collection of my thoughts, poetry and writings that had embedded themselves to my core and now hopefully yours.

Thank you.

Yours,
Emaan Abdul Wahid

About the author.

Emaan Abdul Wahid is an aspiring author who wishes to connect with people on a deeper level, their souls.

She has always had a distinct appreciation for the beauty of art and literature that she started to express through digital art and writing. As the spark of expressing complex emotions through words ignited in her, she has spent day and night scribbling and penning down all the ideas that crossed her mind while drawing art that expressed them, to finally releasing her first ever book, 'remains.'

This is just the beginning of her journey as she wishes to do more literature in the future.

remains- the silent flames that stay untamed

www.ingramcontent.com/pod-product-compliance
Lightning Source LLC
Chambersburg PA
CBHW051455150726
48000CB00005B/2404